Are you pissed? Stressed? Anxious?
Cuss like a sailor?
Like to color? Need motivation?
Then this coloring book is just what
the fuck you need!
No matter what your situation, this
coloring book is sure make you at
least crack a damn smile. Relax,
unwind and color.
And don't be a twat!

Don't be a TWAT

LINT LICKER

hell yes
I
can

Thou shalt not be a CUNT

FUCKING LEGEND

not the day to be a

DICK

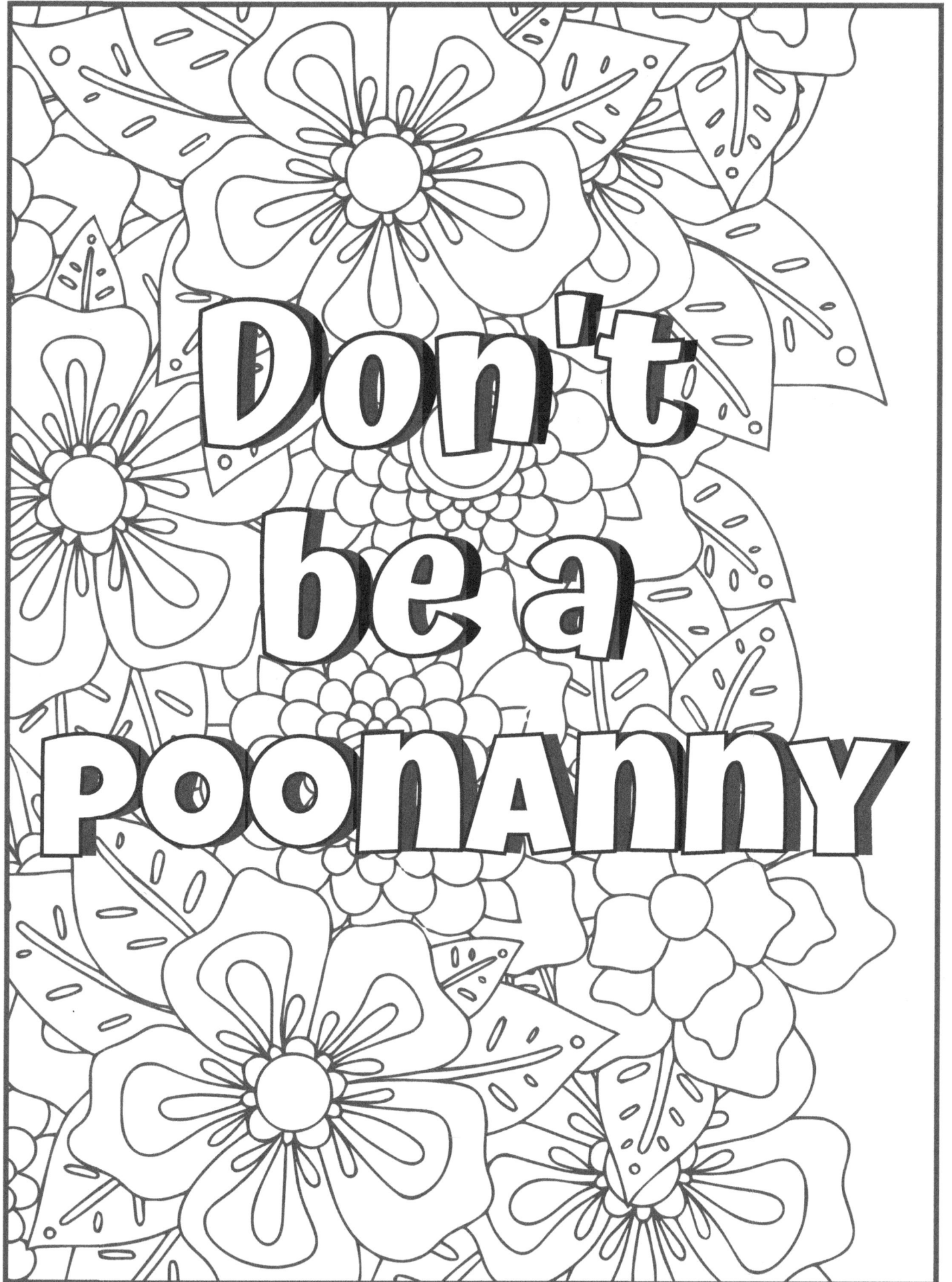

Don't be a Poonanny

ray of *fucking* sunshine

I am a
fucking
QUEEN

DAMN RIGHT I CAN AND I WILL

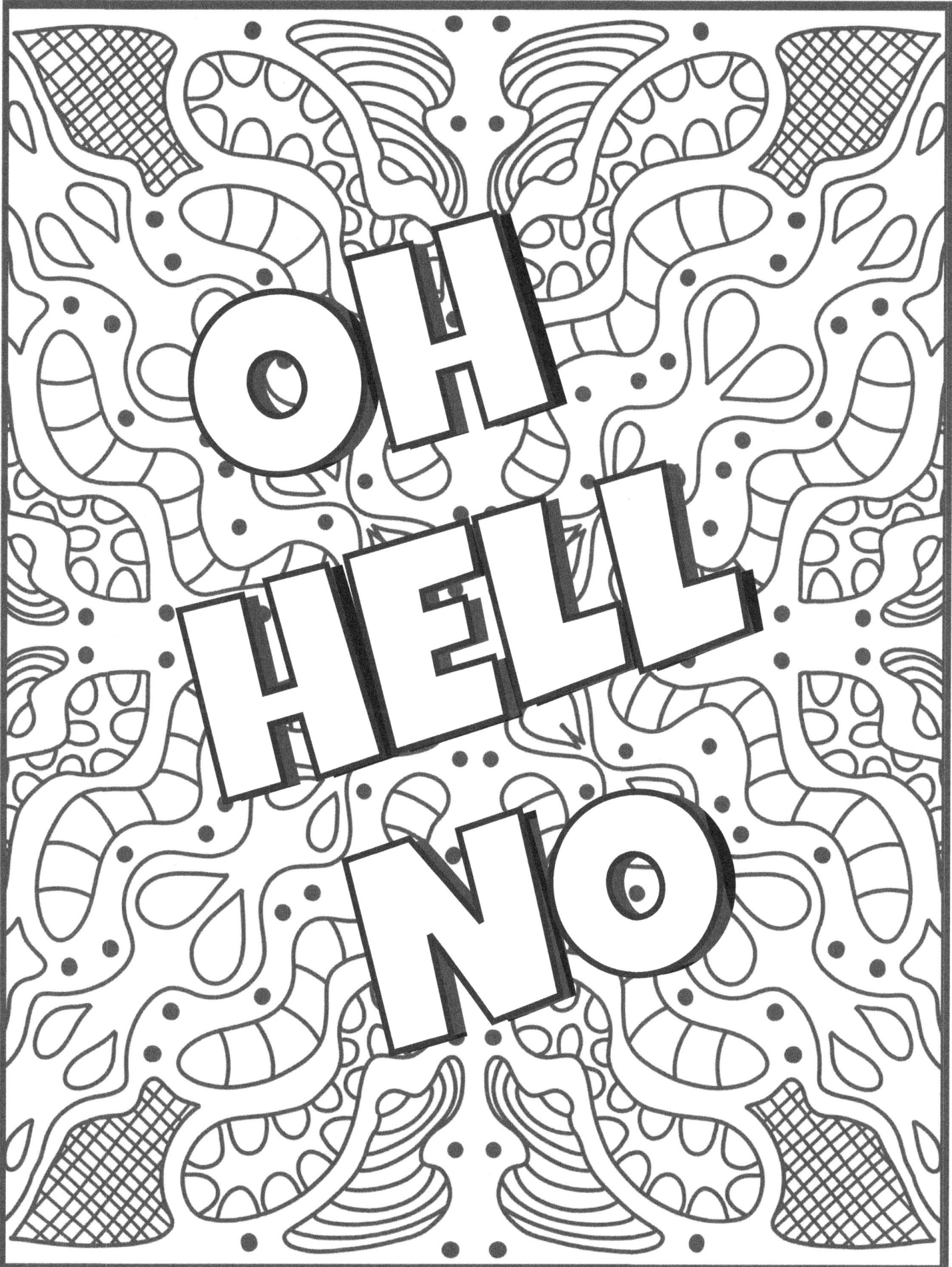

OH HELL NO

you are the
mutha fuckin'
shit

bad bitch

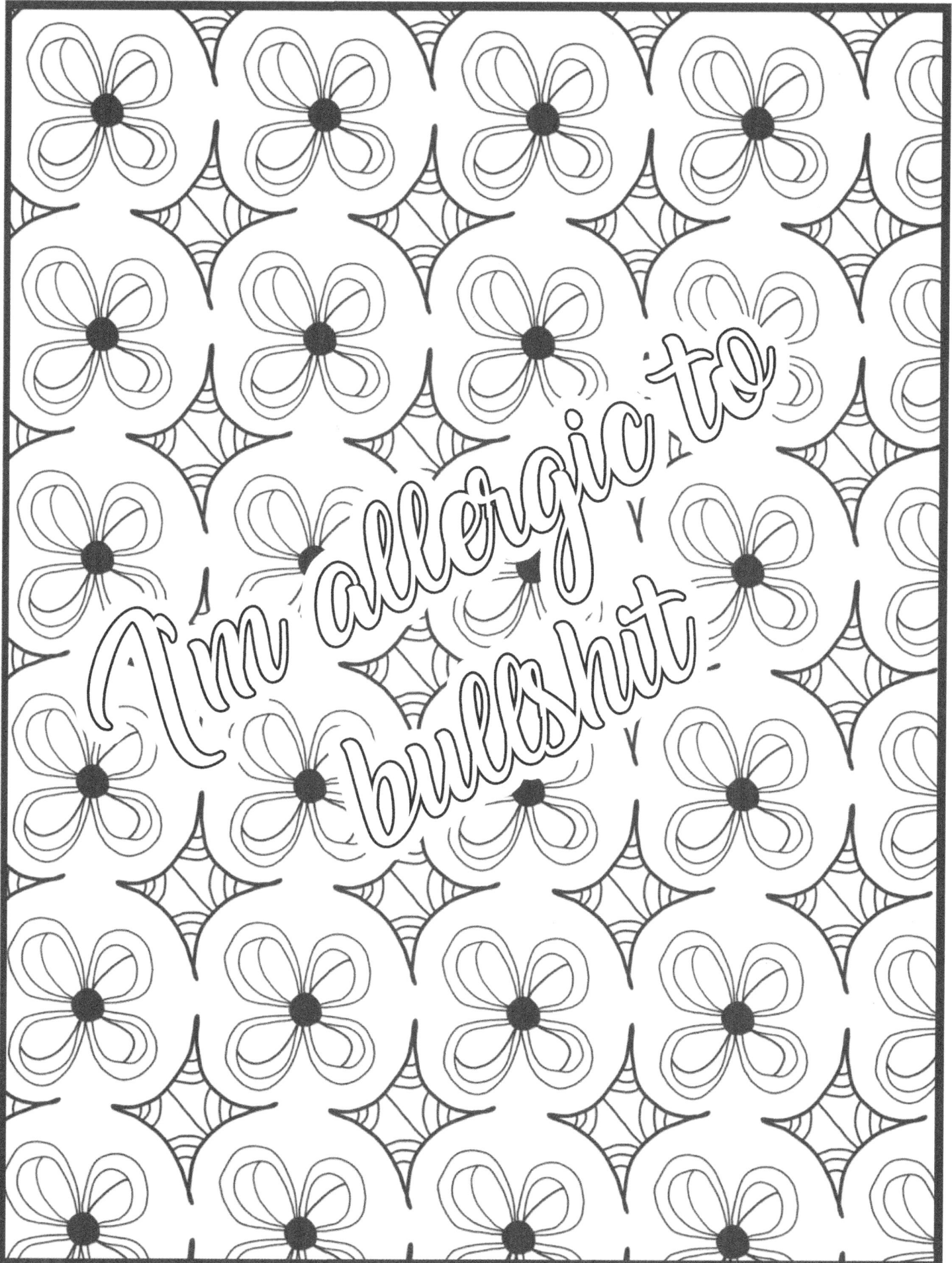

I'm allergic to bullshit

do whatever the fuck you want

TWO WORDS, ONE FINGER

do epic shit

i am
fuckin'
awesome

you fucking got this

fucks I give... none!

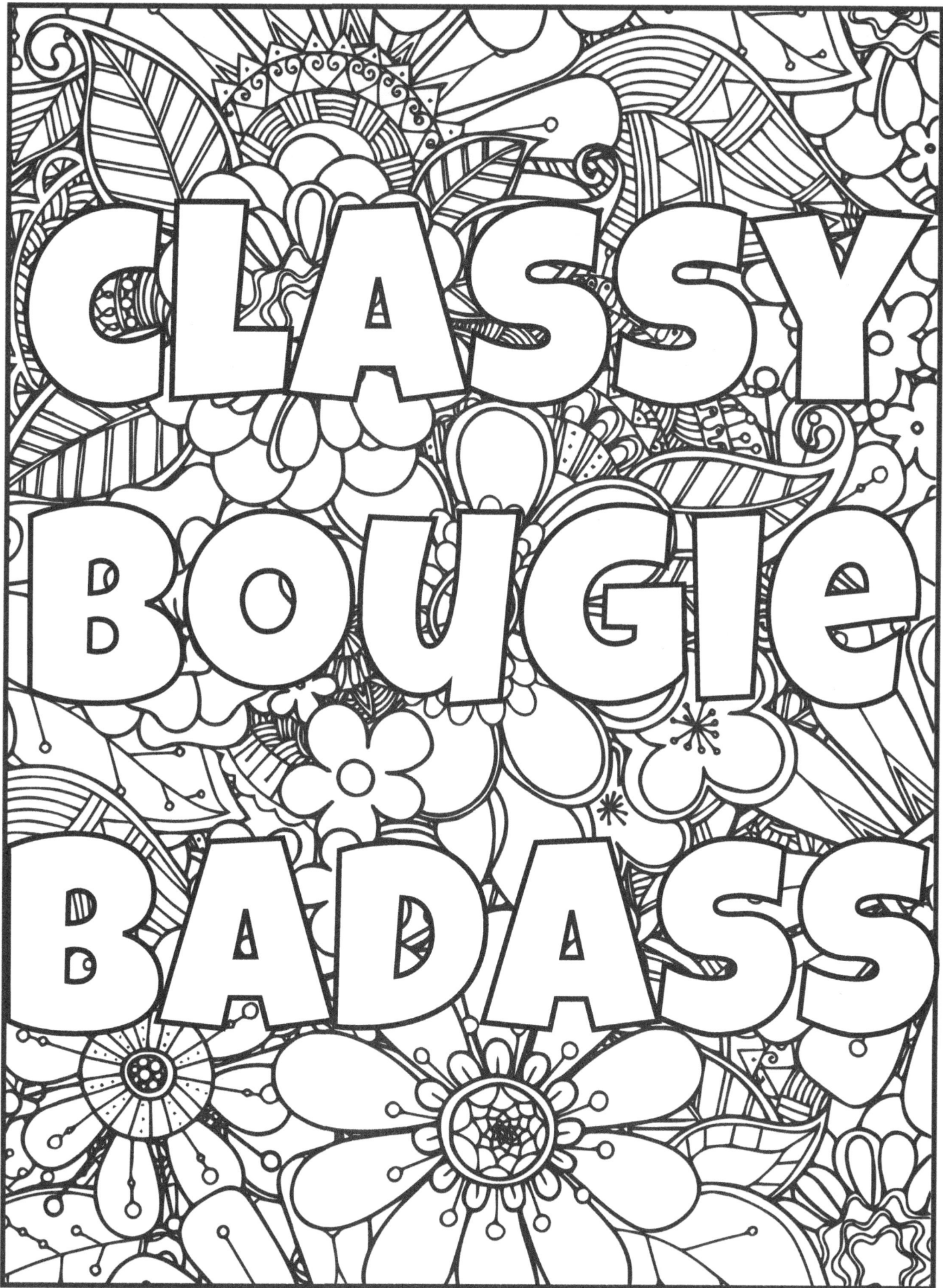

CLASSY BOUGIE BADASS

Damn right I'm worth it

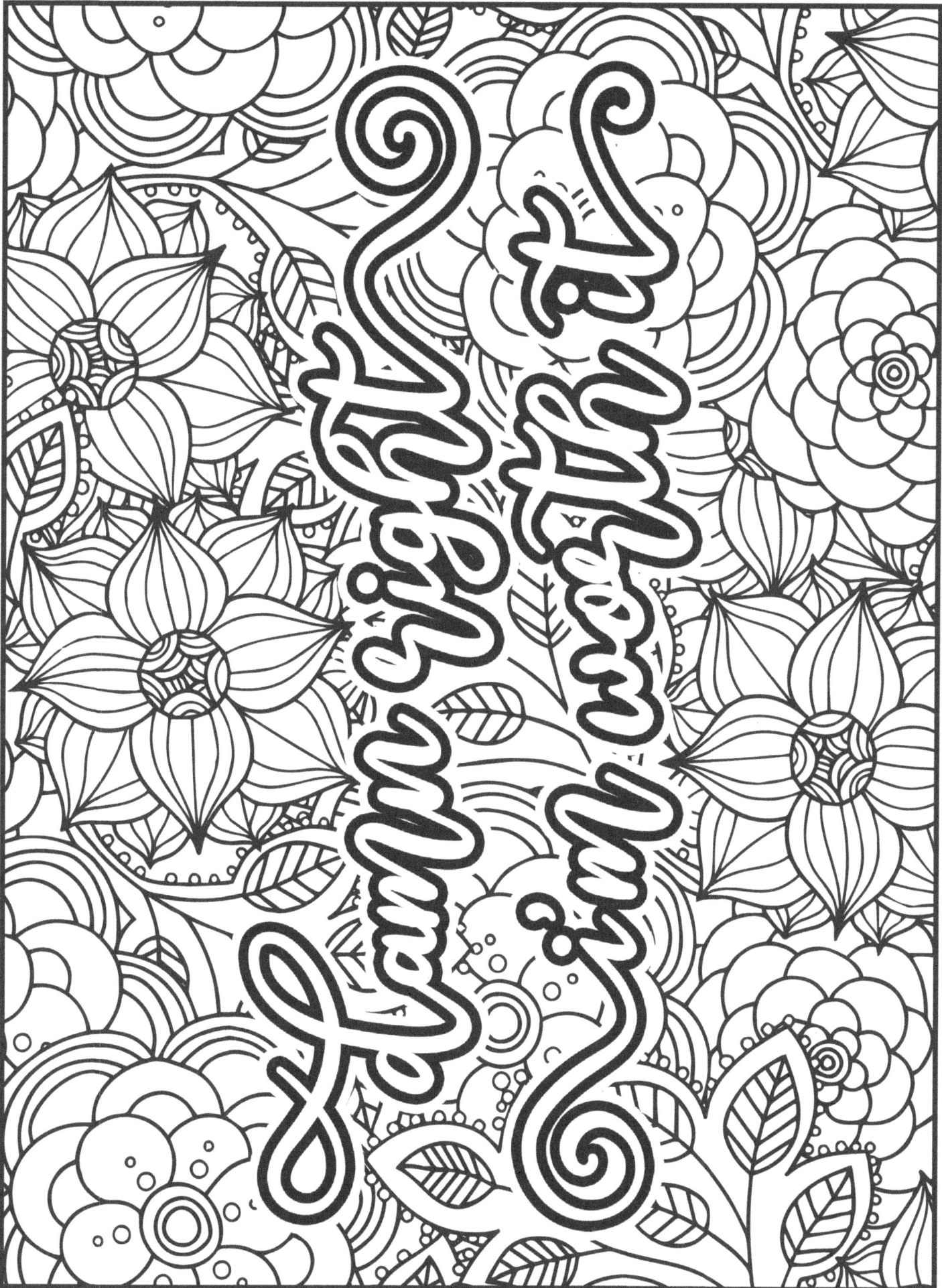